X-pression
Jacqueline James

PUBLISHED by PARABLES
Earthly Stories with a Heavenly Meaning

X-pression
All Rights Reserved to the Author
Jacqueline James

Published By Parables
July, 2019

All Rights Reserved. No part of this book may be reproduced or utilized in any form or by any means, electronic or mechanical, including photocopying, recording, or by any information storage and retrieval system, without permission in writing from the author.

Unless otherwise specified Scripture quotations are taken from the authorized version of the King James Bible.

Readers should be aware that Internet Web sites offered as citations and/or sources for further information may have been changed or disappeared between the time this was written and when it is read.

Illustration provided by www.unsplash.com

ISBN 978-1-945698-20-0

Printed in the United States of America

X-pression
Jacqueline James

PUBLISHED by PARABLES
Earthly Stories with a Heavenly Meaning

Table of Content.

General 44
1. Get to Know You
2. His Wife
3. I Don't Know
4. Something
5. My Own Boss
6. Bye- Bye Girl
7. A Spirit of Confusion
8. Black People
9. Try Me

Spiritual
1. God's Sake
2. My God is Awesome
3. Take the Pain Away
4. His People
5. Deliver Me
6. Servant
7. He's Able
8. After the Storm
9. Your Choice
10. At the Altar
11. Through God's Eyes
12. Get a "Little" Thought

Educational
1. You Are What You Eat
2. Be Comfortable in Your Skin
3. Full Circle
4. Your Addiction
5. Ungrateful

Informative

1. A Virtuous Woman
2. A Friend
3. The Bully
4. Mother's Day
5. Wait Love
6. Because
7. The New Wave Boys
8. Family Love
9. The Beautiful Black Women

Entertainment

1. A Very Hot Day
2. Pretty, Petty, Penny-Pincher
3. Classy, County, Chick
4. I'm Sleepy
5. Bragging, Banging, Bingo, Buddies
6. Back in Time
7. From-the...to-the
8. You Belong
9. Diddy...Wah...Diddy
10. Bunny Rabbit
11. Move the Waste
12. Can't Find Me
13. Talk to Myself
14. Ghetto Twisted

Special Dedication

1. My Friend
2. Baby 'Angel'
3. Message from Heaven
4. Happy Anniversary
5. My Heart
6. New Friend

X-PRESSION

About the Author

Jacqueline James is a published Christian author, who's filled with integrity and humility. Because of her humbleness, she would like to express to her readers' sincere gratitude for purchasing her books.

However, because of her integrity, she would like to express her deepest apology for incorrect information in her first published book "Poetry with a Twist." This incorrect information is contained unintentionally in the "about the author page." It was printed without Jacqueline's knowledge or permission.

You may be wondering how Jacqueline could have possibly missed such significant details. The answer is because she lives in her work. Jacqueline trusted her publisher to do the right thing, by only using the words that she submitted in her manuscript for her "about the author page." Which contained honest and correct information, about her story, that was written by her to be published in her book. Unfortunately, some of the words in that particular page were changed completely, which then made it appear deceitful. By the time Jacqueline realize it was incorrect information, the book had already gone into print. Jacqueline didn't read this false information until months, and two published books later.

Jacqueline is very passionate about her work. Even though her work is written in both fiction and nonfiction, through her poetry, she insists on her audience having the correct information about her life's story.

Jacqueline never gave birth to any children by her first or second husband. After she extended her family to five children, she married her first husband, who perceived her in death. Time passed, then Jacqueline married her second husband which ended in a divorce years later. However, it was not a crucial time in her life when she divorced. God granted her peace, with perseverance to push forward through her journey.

    This information is very important for Jacqueline to express, in the hope to give her readers a sense of her true character. Jacqueline intends for her readers to share with her this amazing journey that God has brought her through. Which will allow them to know through their faith, they also can conquer any and everything, that's set before them.

    Jacqueline believes that God doesn't deal with the pretty and perfect, but God deals with the ugly and imperfections. He turns it into something beautiful, so that He may get the glory from it. Jacqueline continues to express these values daily through her Christian walk.

The Dedication

  This book X-pression is dedicated to my son Centilus Lemont Buchanan. Centilus is a hard-working, loyal young man, who generates tremendous amounts of ambition toward his goals in life. As Centilus strives for his success, he also finds the time to help me. I'm sure that I've instilled a spectacular amount of devotion into him over the years because he projects it through his generosity when keeping me up to speed with the new millennium changes. Centilus is a full-time student who is employed part-time, which demands countless hours of his time. However, Centilus have never once denied me of any of his expertise, when I needed assistance. I truly appreciate his support, and the sacrifices he's made while working with me during this incredible process.

  Thank you Centilus for all the kindness you've shown me. I love you, and I sincerely admire you for the reliable, and self-sufficient man you've become. I also greatly respect how you have continued to stay humble in the process.

X-pression

The Introduction

X-pression is a very influential book of poetry designed to enhance the reader's perspective on different emotions that may arrive doing everyday life encounters. This book will allow its readers to channel those emotions, and comfortably express them with confidence. It was intentionally written for its readers to see themselves through both problematic and pleasant situations.

Its primary objective is to express the similarities throughout all nationalities when facing both challenging, and pleasurable circumstances. The author hopes that the readers obtain the knowledge to face those challenging situations and conquered them in a productive manner. It was carefully crafted through poetry to soothe its readers into the acceptance of change. The author desire is to express some spiritual awareness through the essence of her poetry. She also intends to fill the readers with useful information, while entertaining them, therefore, leaving them with a positive collection of thoughts.

X-PRESSION

Chapter 1
General
1. Get to Know you
2. His Wife
3. I Don't Know
4. Something
5. My Own Boss
6. Bye-Bye Girl
7. A Spirit of Confusion
8. Black People
9. Try me

Get to Know You...

Now that I have a moment of your time;
I'm going to stop, and give you mine:
I'm going to get to know you, and pick your brain;
Steal your secrets, and drive you insane:
Just wait a moment, I need to get this right;
So, I don't stay awake wondering all night:
What's your motive, what's on your mind?
I need to know if your thoughts are kind:
What's your angle? Where are you coming from?
Are you in this just for fun?
If you're not committed, then that's fine;
But, don't be over here wasting my time:
Give me a reason to want you around;
I don't need you to cramp my style:
This is not a joke this thing's for real;
Now, I need to know just how you feel:
I'm not going to stay here talking for long;
Trying to figure out what's going on
Now, I have some questions I want to ask;
So be honest, and try your best:
I need to know what your intentions are;
Are you serious, or just trying to score?
I'm taking the time to get to know you;
And, I believe it's the best thing to do.

His Wife...

If you are a star from high above;
And he's the light that shone below,
Then I'm that spark that caught the glow!

If you are the sea that filled the land;
And he's the wave that fluttered through,
Then I'm the dampness and moisture that grew!

If you are the space all around,
And he's the time that filled it;
Then I'm the hour to measure it with!

If you are a tree tall and strong,
And he's the roots that spread to the ground;
Then I'm the oxygen that formed around:

Since you are a mother, God sent to bear a seed,
And he's the seed that formed to life;
Then I'm the one to serve as his wife.

I Don't Know...

I don't know what's going on;
I just want you to move along:
If you don't know what you're doing, stop wasting my time;
Get someone who does, then that'll be fine:
Quit faking like you know 'this' when you're wrong
as two left shoes;
After you messed up the entire job, then I get the bad news:
You refuse to quit;
Even though you couldn't handle it:
And you left everything ruined;
Because you didn't know what you were doing:
But, I'm not supposed to fuss;
After you broke up all my stuff:
Did you think it wasn't going to matter;
If you couldn't make it better?
Don't walk away, like you're insane;
Own up to what you did, and stop playing games;
I don't know why are you trying to salvage the remains;
Because, you're going to pay for all of 'this,' just the same:
I don't know what you came to do;
But, we both know the 'job,' wasn't right for you:
But, you faked like you were qualified;
And, the whole day has been one fat lie:
Now, you're in my face, talking about "where's my pay?"
Man you owe me for my stuff, and the rest of my day!

Something...

It's always something that's going to make you laugh,
and make you blush;
Or make you fuss or make you hush:
Something to make you cry, or make you sigh;
Something to give you the will to live, and not to die:
Something to make you love, or make you care;
Something to give you the courage not to fear:

Something to work hard for, or hardly work;
Something to empower you, or make you a jerk:
Something to make you hot, or to make you cold;
Something to keep you calm, or make you bold:
Something to make you hungry, or to make you full;
Something to make you notice when you hear "bull,"
Something to be inspired by, or make you proud;
Something to make you pleased, or shout out loud:
Something to motivate you, or keep you going;
Something to inform others of what you're doing:

Something to keep you cautious, before you make a mistake;
Something that keeps you strong, from the crap you take:
Something that keeps you smart, and wise beyond your time;
Something that keeps you quiet, with a peace of mind:
Something that makes you happy in your time of sorrow;
Something that makes you smile through your tomorrow:
Something to make you go, or make you stay;
Something to make you worship, or make you pray:

X-PRESSION

Something to make you watch, or let you see;
Something to keep you driven, until your soul's free:
Something that gives you hope in the midst of your storm;
Something that gives you a sense of norm:
Something to give you comfort, and keep you safe;
Something to help you find your perfect place.

My Own Boss...

I work from home so that I can be my own boss;
Good or bad, I pay the cost:
When I get on my nerves, I pay myself no attention;
The stress from the workplace, I don't have to mention:
I pay myself, so I can fire me, or give me a raise;
And when I'm tired, I sleep in, and just have lazy days:
One good thing about it all, I make my own dress code;
I can come to work in my PJs, or nothing at all and be bold:
I often promote myself to 'General Former';
Then, I demote myself, so I no longer have to work for me:
Sometimes I overwork me, because of my dedication;
And there are other times when I give myself a break,
and even a mini-vacation:
When I get a headache, I take a sick day and sleep in;
And who's going to tell on me? I'm my own best friend:
The hardest thing I had to do,
was save for my own retirement;
I hide my shares from myself, then I go back and find them:
I give me all the overtime I want,
but my wages stay the same;
But, when I complain to the boss, I'm calling my own name:
I can't even lay-me-off, or draw unemployment,
even if I fire me:
The only thing I can possibly do, is
scream at the person who hired me!

Bye-Bye Girl...

Alright, I'm gone;
I'll be back, and it won't be long:
I'll be back before ten, and I'll be ready to go again:
I'm the bye-bye, girl; I thought you knew;
Everywhere I go, is somewhere new:
I'm on the go, day, and night:
Sometimes, I don't return until the morning light:
I'm always out; I'm always gone;
I'm never there, cause I'm never home:
I like to go, and I like to roam;
Whatever I lay my purse, is my home:
If you need me, call my phone;
And if not, just leave me alone:
I'll be there when I come;
I'm out right now, having fun:
I go up and down the road;
And, it doesn't ever get old:
Don't stay up waiting on me;
I'll be back, you'll see:
There is no need to pout;
I'm just out, and about:
I'm the bye-bye girl;
And, I'm trying to see the world.

A Spirit of Confusion...

A spirit of confusion, to draw its own conclusion;
Demonic spirits are everywhere;
They possess the ones that don't even care:
The power is great if you allow it in;
But please be aware, they're not your friend:
They come in your presence, with bad intentions;
Only to distract you, and get your attention:
They're never calm, or at peace;
Their happiness for life has already decreased:
They're very miserable, and need your company;
To make sure, that your life is also interrupted:
They come around with hostility, and confusion;
Because, they're empty, as a broken loser:
They always have something negative to say;
Especially, when everyone's having a good day:
And, don't let them around, if you're feeling bad;
Because they'll make sure that your day is miserable and sad:
They'll condemn the things that you stand for;
And, they're never going to be on the same accord:
There's never any pleasing them at all;
They don't want to see you get ahead just fall:
Their characteristics of filled with jealousy, and hate;
When they see something good, they refused to participate:
They disrupt other lives because they can;
But, refuse to take responsibilities like a woman or man:
They try to get inside of your head;
And, corrupt your thoughts until your dead:

X-PRESSION

They're never satisfied, nor are they content;
Because, they don't understand about the Son,God sent:
They haven't accepted the love, that Jesus gives;
To bless their days as they live:
And, because of that, they're miserable and mad;
And, they try to block your joy, to make you sad:
They have a spirit of confusion;
And, it's only satisfied when chaos is the conclusion.

Black People...

I'm having fun with "my people," we have different shades
of black skin;
We're filled with lots of love, and greatness within:
We're a multi-talented race of people;
Our skills, are what complete us:
I enjoy mingling with my kind;
Their spirits are compatible to mine:
It'll take some time to understand;
How crafty we are with our hands:
Our spirits rage up high;
To meet our dreams in the sky:
We've overcome the impossible odds;
That separates us from the crowd:
Our skin is dark, but our souls are bright;
Keeping us inspired, to continue to fight:
Our struggles are hard, and the battles are long;
That's what builds our character, and keeps us strong:
We're filled with 'spunk', and blessed with a gift;
That keeps us peaceful, when our life's shift:
We're filled with rhythm, and with dance;
Keeping us balanced, as we work our hands:
We're a breeding race, that keeps generations going;
Breeding brilliance, and it's forever growing:
I enjoy being with my people of color;
Identifying the women as my mother:
I came out to be with all 'blacks' in the house;
Cause we are the beginning, and Jesus paid our cost!

Try Me...

Don't mess with me; I'll drop you off;
You're truly rude, now hush your mouth:
You'll end up walking from the north to the south;
If you keep on running, your big fat mouth:
You're getting on my nerves, so shut up now;
Don't you say a word, don't make a sound:
The tone of your voice is bothering me;
So, please be quiet and let me be:
Now, you want to threaten me;
You need a dose of reality:
You're talking to me all ratchet, and insane;
You think this is some type of twisted game:
Try me, try me, try me please;
I'll knock you down, and make you bleed:
I'll make you wish we never met;
And, that's not a threat, that's a fact:
I think it's time to put you out;
So, you will know what life's about:
Since you think you can say anything you like;
While you're riding in my car, in the middle of the night:
So, say something else, please feel free;
Just open your mouth, go ahead and try me!

Chapter 2
Spiritual

1. God's Sake
2. My God is Awesome
3. Take the Pain Away
4. His People
5. Deliver Me
6. Servant
7. He's Able
8. After the Storm
9. Your Choice
10. At the Altar
11. Through God's Eyes
12. Get a "Little" Thought

God's Sake...

Nature's own, for God sake;
You can rest assured; he didn't make a mistake:
He identifies with everything we say and do;
God 'weeds' out the bad, and holds on to a few:
Many may be called, but only a few will be chosen;
The ones who understood, why Jesus rose:

God's mercy endures "from-time-to-come,"
That's the reason he sent his Son!
For those who worship, and believe;
In Jesus name, they will achieve:
Their lives will be covered under his blood;
Because they're filled with Jesus' love:
They understand the mercy God gives;
To carry their burdens as they live:
They trust in the power of the Holy Ghost;
To give them healing, for the most:
Throughout their lives, they will be tested;
But, if they fulfill the prophecy, they will be blessed:
These are God's people, who are highly favored;
Because, of their struggle, and their labor:
They have faced obstacles, and went through the storm;

And, came out more than a conqueror in Jesus' arms:
With all of their heart, God's word they embraced;
And, waited diligently, to see their Father's face:
These are the soldiers, who God chose to make;
Who fought for righteousness, for God's sake.

X-PRESSION

My God is Awesome...

My God is awesome; he heals me when I'm sick;
He gives me strength when I'm weak:
He blesses me when I'm down;
He keeps me with a smile:

My God is awesome; he helps me during the day;
He blesses me when I pray;
He dries up all my tears;
He comforts me through my fears:

My God is awesome; he watches over me at night;
He lets me see his light:
He shelters me through my storm;
He cradled me safely in his arms:

My God is awesome; he supplies all my needs;
I feel the love he brings;
He helps me in my life;
I'm healed through Jesus stripes:

My God is awesome; he gives me peace of mind;
With his grace, I'm fine;
He died on a cross, but rose again;
To forgive me for my sins:

My God is awesome; the only friend I know;
He's with me as I go:
He removed the shackles from my feet;
He lifted my burdens, so I am free:

My God is awesome; he keeps me satisfied;
And his mercy, he doesn't deny:
My God is awesome; he keeps my spirit free:
My God is awesome; he helps me to believe:
My God is awesome; he covers me with his blood:
My God is awesome; I can feel my Father's love.

Take the Pain Away...

I would like to take your pain away, but I can't;
I can't take your pain away;
But, I can kneel beside you, and pray:
There is a man by the name of Jesus;
And this man died, for that very reason!
He'll make sure there's no pain left;
But, you must call on Him for yourself:
There's no other name ever given before;
Who laid down His life for every woman, man, girl, and boy:
He died to save us, whether we wanted it, or not;
He laid down His life, to bring us all out!

Out of confusion, misery, and pain;
But, you must open your mouth, and call on Jesus' name:
He died for the hopeless, inflicted, and despaired;
Just call His name, and he'll be with you everywhere:
He died for the fatherless, the weary, and the lonely
He wants to be your savior, and your only:
He died for the widowers, and those who are heavily burdened;
When you call the name Jesus, you'll be comforted for certain:
Jesus can take your pain away and bring about peace, throughout
your day:

He gives you hope, He'll bring you joy,
and He'll fill you with peace;
And the pain you felt, will cease:
Jesus will take the pain away, and you will be relieved;
If you trust in Him, and just believe.

His People...

Created in His image are His people;
Worshipping together in His steeple:
Loving the sound of Jesus' word;
The saints are the sweetest voices to be heard:
Giving Him praise as they sing;
Filled with the love, that Jesus' bring:
Blessed are the ones who call His name;
Through their worship and their praise:
Giving Him honor for their day;
Lifting Him up as they pray:
His people have faith, and they believe;
In the power of the Holy Ghost, to achieve:
Their lives are rich with Jesus' love;
And, they're protected under his blood:
In this world, they know their place;
Because they're blessed through Jesus' grace:
It's truly an honor to be a saint;
Throughout the day, they show restraint:
They're humble, and they have a lot to give;
Through their actions, Jesus' spirit lives:
And, because of it, the world will know;
They represent Jesus wherever they go.

Deliver Me…

Deliver me, Lord, from myself;
I only want your will to be left:
Deliver me from my wasteful needs;
Lord remove my shackles, I ask you please:
I want to give you my very best;
I desire deliverance, to pass my test:
Lord deliver me from any wicked ways;
Bless my soul, throughout my days:
Lord deliver me from all unpleasant thoughts;
Deliver me Jesus, bring me out:
Deliver me from all things unseen;
Refill me with the joy, you bring:
Free my soul, and cleanse my mind;
Deliver me until your peace, I'll find:
Deliver me from my worldly desires;
Change my heart, and set my soul on fire:
Lord as my flesh do pass away;
Keep my soul, until my deliverance day:
Lord when you call upon my name;
Deliver me first, so I don't remain the same:
Lord make me righteous, before the King;
With deliverance, my praises to Him, I sing.

Servant...

I serve the Lord, and I serve others:
I'm a servant, and I get it from my mother:
I come from a long generation of Christians;
Who was led by a sanctified mission:
They had the Lord's word stored in their heart;
Because, of their faithfulness, His love will never part:
They served God throughout their days;
They prayed, they worshiped, and gave God their praise:

Because of our traditions, I'm blessed today;
God hears my cry when I begin to pray:
I pray my lips don't call him in vain,
When I serve under Jesus' name,

I do what my Lord asks of me;
And, in my obedience the world does see:
I'm his servant, and I'll do his will;
And, throughout my days his love, I feel:
I help his people along the way;
I show them that healing, comes when they pray:
I show them how to serve the Lord by their own choice;
And, how to praise gracefully, as they lift their voice:
Then, we fellowship together, on one accord;
Worshiping together faithfully, serving Our Lord!

He's Able...

I worship, and pray all day long;
In between writing a beautiful song:
Each piece more desirable, than the one before;
Which is filled with the love, my Father, gives to adore:
God has made things possible for me to see;
And, through His grace, He humbles me:
I'm blessed, and I know it, and through my writing, I show it;
As long as I'm able, I'll continue writing, in His favor:
The most wonderful thing, I must say;
Through God's grace, I can see another day:
My songs are coming from above;
I thank God, for all his love!
I'm happy, and I'm content;
From all the gifts our Father, sent:
Because of my faith our Father was able;
To bless me with a gift, and showed me favor:
God is able to wake me up each morning;
Because He does I give Him the glory,
My Lord is able to keep me clothed in my right state of mind;
And I thank Him for it, because I'm doing fine:
Jesus kept my mind on Him, throughout my day;
And He blessed me greatly along my way:
With my whole heart, I do believe, that God is able to supply all
my needs: Because, of it, I share my story;
As I lift my voice to give God the glory!

After the Storm...

After every storm there is a rainbow;
Those who trust in your name will always know:
The harder the struggle, the greater the show;
And, I'm living proof, that blessings do grow:
The blessing comes, when you're humble and meek;
And, show love, to the people you meet:
We all have situations to overcome;
And, God makes us stronger, when we're done:
He'll give you strength for your life to exceed;
If you have faith in Jesus and believe:
Your struggle will be lifted, and your load will be lighter;
When you put your trust in Jesus your days will be brighter:
There's always a rainbow after the storm;
To let you know, you're in God's arms:
The rainbow will be bright enough, for the world to see;
It's beauty was meant to be a blessing to you and me.

Your Choice...

Your body may be weak, tired and old;
But, your faith in Jesus will restore your soul;
Jesus doesn't want your human flesh;
He just wants to use your spirit,
In time your flesh will fade away;
And your human body will soon decay:
But, our minds are something we can control;
They can live forever with Jesus, or in satan's hole:
Our soul's resting place is just a conscious choice;
We're given redemption when we express our voice:
So, call on the name of Jesus, for any reason;
He'll be there during every season:
God has breathed life into your soul;
Now, you must choose Jesus to take control:
If you want to be prosperous and live your life blessed;
Then, give your life to Jesus, and he'll take care of the rest:
We're all given the choice to do what's right;
When we choose Jesus, he'll lead us to our Father's light.

At the Altar...

Leave your burdens at the altar,
Our Lord and Savior died for the cost of them:
Your breakthrough is on the other side;
God has prepared a place for your spirit to reside:
However, you must sacrifice;
To live a righteous life,
You must give up some things;
If you want to receive the glory God brings;
God wants our hearts to be pure;
So, give up your worldly desires if you're sure:
God is here to heal our bodies, and save our souls;
When we trust in him to take control,

If you have sickness in your body and need it to be healed:
Leave it at the altar in prayer, God's word is real:
If you're anxious, worried, or depressed;
Leave at the altar in prayer to be blessed:
If you're lonely, sad, or confused;
Leave it at the altar, and wait for God's good news:
If you're mistreated, disappointed, or your heart breaks;

Leave it at the altar, for heaven sakes:
If you're unemployed, without, or just poor;
Leave it at the altar, God will deliver you from it, and more:
If you have an addiction or any type of affliction;
Leave it at the altar; God has no restrictions:
If your body is weary, weak and tired;
Leave it at the altar; it's the reason our Savior died.

Through God's Eyes...

I see the lies of demons, through God's eyes;
Their evil comes to me, as no surprise:
I have the shield of righteousness on my side;
They hide behind their idols, and false pride:
They are intimidated by my very presence;
I hold the key to life-long lessons:
They may be possessed and the masters of deception;
However, I have wisdom and very keen perception:
They wear masks and all types of disguises;
But, with my detection I'm able to recognize,

You can run, but you can't hide, there's nowhere to go;
Your covers with shatter and your true identity will show:
I have long seen you, before the beginning of time;
The secrets you possess have all fluttered through my mind;
I represent truth, which is sometimes hard to find,
I sense your malice when you are near;
Your devious motives are very clear:
I feel your intent; I know your purpose;
You do not fool me, and that's for certain:
My eyes pierce right through, all your shame:
Your secrets unfold, and the truth remains,
I'm able to see you, through God's eyes,
This makes me blessed, and very wise.

JACQUELINE JAMES

Get a "Little" Thought...

Get a little thought here;
And get a little thought there:
Just remember that God is for you, and He's everywhere:
Now, that I have your attention;
I just stopped by to mention:
As, I sing with praise, and lift my voice;
You'll all know that Jesus is the right choice:
From every nationality and walks of life;
Must believe that Jesus died to pay our price:
He hung on the cross, and shed His blood;
So, the entire world would know his love:
You must accept him as your Savior, by your own free will;
And a blessed and holy life you will live:
Give him your all, that's what he wants;
To control your life, and that's being blunt:
He'll keep your mind in perfect peace;
As your faith in him continue to increase:
When you open your heart for Jesus to come in;
He'll be closer than any family, or friend:
For any sins, you might've done before;
Jesus forgives you, it won't matter anymore:
You're a new creature in Christ, once you repent;
To forgive the world is why Jesus was sent:
Just a little thought here; And a little thought there:
God will show you how much He cares.

X-pression

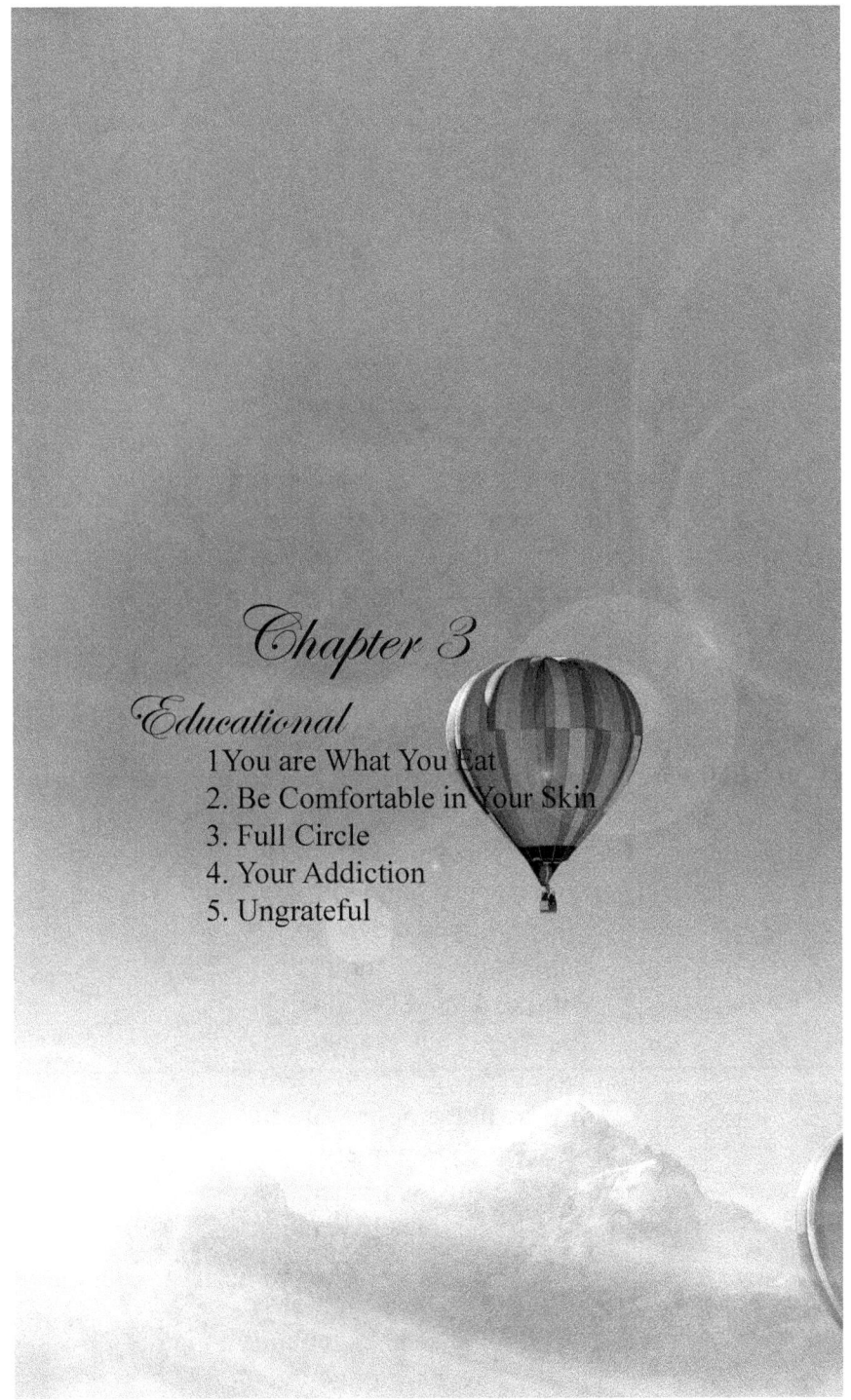

Chapter 3
Educational
1. You are What You Eat
2. Be Comfortable in Your Skin
3. Full Circle
4. Your Addiction
5. Ungrateful

X-PRESSION

You are What You Eat...

I want to be the calcium from the cheese;
And the vitamins from the green beans:
But I'm sitting with a bad back;
Cause I'm the junk, from all the snacks:
Am I going to run wild like an animal, from eating their meat?
Or will I be sweet, from all the candy I eat:
Will I just sit around and doodle?
From eating only pasta and noodles:
Will I swim deep in the water, with my hips, if I only eat fish and shrimp? Now can I tell the doctor good-bye?
Cause I'm the "apple of his eye,"
If I only eat sugar and spice;
Will it really make me nice?
If I eat only sausages and pepperoni;
Will I end up being lonely?
I think I'm going to eat, potatoes and steak;
But I won't stay up, eating them late,
I won't eat all the pastry and cake;
So I won't end up overweight:
I'm going to eat the dairy and the fruit;
So I'll end up being cute:
Give me all the vegetables and peas;
So, I'll end up healthy, please!
I want to eat the foods that keep me strong;
Then I'll know I won't go wrong.

Be Comfortable in Your Skin...

Always be comfortable in your skin;
That alone will allow you to win:
Once everything's said and done, be happy with yourself;
Because when it's all over it'll only be you left,
Fight hard for your 'right' to be here;
Make your voice count so that the entire world could hear:
Set boundaries but, make no limitations;
Rise above everyone's expectations:
It's not about your race;
Or the color of your face;
It's all about your heart;
So, please do your part:
Be comfortable in your skin, regardless of your circumstances;
Your life is about your struggle,
and your willingness to take chances:
Make your situation work for you;
Give it your all, and do the best that you can do:
Once it's good in your heart, and you're satisfied;
Either the world will accept it, or it might be denied;
Nevertheless, give it your best effort as you try:
Regardless of anything, master your faith before you die:

X-PRESSION

Push yourself, so that you're able to rise above;
And you'll have blessings through Jesus' unconditional love:
We don't always get two legs or even arms;
But we still must work diligently with whatever comes:
Believe in our own ability to succeed;
And with the grace of God, you will achieve:
So, keep your head up as you proceed;
And your faith will keep you strong, you must believe:
So, regardless if you're fat, white, black, or thin;
Just be comfortable in your skin.

JACQUELINE JAMES

Full Circle...

We're in this full circle, trying desperately to get free;
It goes around and around for years, and if you're not careful,
you'll keep bumping into me,
We're like a bunch of rats in a maze, looking for the cheese;
But, the way out is success, to meet our needs:
If you keep running into the same people years later over again;
Then you've never gone anywhere if they weren't your friend:
If you're trying to get ahead, to find a way out;
Then you're trapped in a circle, without a doubt.

I came across a lady from my past;
She said that we went to school together, and she was in my class:
I looked at her face; however I didn't recognize her at all;
She told stories of things we did up and down the halls,
She started to speak as if I knew;
And, continued to talk, but I still didn't remember it,
her when she was through:
So, I played it off, as if I've been there;
I wanted to say that I've been all over the world,
yet I hadn't gone anywhere:

We both stood there with a casual smile;
Wanting to know desperately about the other's style:
I then deported with a blank look;
I was in this circle, with part of my past took:

X-PRESSION

Had I done anything, to prove I was alive,
If I continue to run into the same old jive?
I try to block it out, and I try to forget;
That I'm trapped in a maze, that I haven't escaped yet:
I'm running in a full circle, like a rat looking for cheese:
Just, going through life, waiting for success, please!

Your Addiction...

For all you alcoholics, and drug addicts trying to get
past that stage;
Stop counting your days, and be about your praise,
All things good, God will fulfill;
Just keep your faith, and give in, to his will,
He'll get you past, whatever you're struggling with;
He'll give you hope, and the strength to quit:
If you're struggling with addiction throughout your day;
Then ask God to help you with it, when you pray:
Just trust in Jesus, and you will see;
He'll break bad habits, and you'll be free:
He'll give you the strength to bring you out;
And, you'll be clean and sober, without a doubt:
So, just try him for yourself;
I assure you that you won't need nothing else:
He will cleanse your body, from your head to your toe;
You'll become a new creature through Christ,
and everyone will know:
Your load will be lifted, and resolved overnight;
And, your days will be happier, as you follow Jesus' light:
The days will come, and the days will go;
And, you'll soon realize, that you don't need the drugs,
or alcohol any more:
Regardless of the meetings, or any rehab;
You'll stay clean and sober when you follow God's path.

Ungrateful...

The more you do for some children,
the more ungrateful they become;
As, soon as they get an opportunity, out the door they run:
You showed them love, and gave them discipline,
And, you taught them right from wrong, and instilled principals:
They rebelled against your rules,
and when you try to put them in their place;
They slammed the door on the way out and "spit in your face!"
If you tell them to do their chores- wash the dishes,
or make the bed;
They act as if you've done them wrong, or went upside their head:
The more you give, the more they want;
And it doesn't matter if you've done your part:
You can make sure they're fed, and give them their way;
And drive them to school faithfully, every school day,
You can dress them up nicely, and take them on family outings,
and show them your best;
And they'll look at you ungratefully,
and asked, "Where is the rest?"
They never went without shelter, gas, electric, water, or food:
And always had toys to play with, clean clothes, and new shoes:
They had their own bouncy house,
water slide, and swimming pool;
And, they could play on it as long as
they wanted on summer afternoons:

You took them sledding in the winter time,
and had lots of snowball fights;
You dressed them warm, and played in the snow
until the day lost its light:
They went to amusement parks with swings, roller coasters, and
merry-go-rounds;
At the end of the day, they had so much fun
they hardly made a sound:
They went on field trips to the zoo, and learned about animals all
around the world;
They went to the Science Center to learn about different elements
of the earth such as zinc, copper, diamonds, and pearls:
You join the YMCA so, they can take swimming lessons;
You enroll them in dance classes, and even gymnastics;
They took martial arts, marched in the band,
and played various sports;
You spent lots of money, volunteered your time, and supported
them from the heart:
You took vacations, went to church, and instilled Christian values;
You read to them, helped them study,
And taught them valuable lessons:
You supported their dreams, to make them
feel the best that they could be;
However, they didn't appreciate it, and couldn't wait
to move out to be free:
Unfortunately, some children create their own stress;
Instead of accepting their situation, and
realizing that they're blessed:
Sometimes, they must be removed from their comfort zone;
To appreciate that they had a good home:
They'll move out but won't have a glorious story to share;
But us as parents won't lose any sleep, or lose, any of our hair:
These are the ungrateful children that think you owe them more;
These are the children that disrespect you, on the way out the door.

Chapter 4

Information

1. A Virtuous Woman
2. A Friend
3. The Bully
4. Mother's Day
5. Wait Love
6. Because
7. The New Wave Boys
8. Family Love
9. The Beautiful Black Women

A Virtuous Woman…

A Virtuous Woman…
A virtuous woman never lays down until her work is done;
And, she's up again at the dust of dawn;
She only decides to turn off the lights;
When her work for the day is completed right:
Her family (if any), are satisfied;
Before the end of her day, and she closes her eyes:
The chores are done, and her house is clean;
And she's not confrontational, nor is she mean:
She's firm with her discipline but easy on the tongue;
She's well-rounded, and charismatic, but fun:
Her personality inspires you, to be a better person;
She's always compassionate, and that's for certain:
She has strong Christian values and is very mink;
She shows humility, but she's not weak:
She has plenty of wisdom, through experience and age;
Living peacefully is how she spends her days:
She handles business on every level;
The intelligent she possesses will inspire generations forever:
She's loyal and worthy with great convictions;
She embraces the world with limited restrictions:
Her dedication goes pass any of our understanding;
She gives the utmost respect, and also demands it:
She's earnest and hardworking;
Yet, gentle and nurturing:

She's a very honest person, and fun to be around;
And her witty ways, makes her stand out in a crowd:
As a friend, she's the best; you'll never need another;
And she's great as a wife and a fantastic mother:
Now, you're thinking to yourself, "Who could this possibly be?"
No need to look any further, the answer is me!

A Friend...

Today I met an acquaintance, that turned into a friend;
My heart was heavily loaded, and she had a listening ear to lend:
As I started to speak, I could tell that she was down to earth;
And, at that very moment, I began to smirk:
We sat and talked for hours, under the shaded light;
And, I didn't decide to leave, until the bugs began to bite:
Some of the subjects were personal and sensitive to discuss;
But, when we talked about her family, she didn't put up a fuss:
That made me feel comfortable to open-up my thoughts;
I began to break the rules that I was initially taught:
I know we formed a bond, that won't be easily broken;
I'm sure she felt it as well after I had spoken:
The laughs were our connection, as we united;
And, the peace that was left among us, was more than invited:
I'm glad I took the time to get to know her better;
And, when we speak again, it won't be in a letter:
Because of all her kindness, that she was willing to lend;
I hope she knows I'm grateful, and
she's worthy of being called a friend:
I invited her to my home to "break bread," with me:
And I will be able to show her my hospitality.

The Bully...

I knew it immediately, when you spoke,
as you walk through the door;
Your tongue is sharper than a two-headed sword:
It's like a ninja star with blades all around;
Waiting on the next victim to bring down,
You cut people down by belittling their name;
And, when the next person comes you treat them the same:
And, if someone comes and voice their opinion;
You become confrontational and we all know who's winning:
I was told to stay far away and clear from your path;
Not to come in contact, just let others speak on my behalf:
But, I know your kind, I've seen it before;
If I stood up to you, you won't be so tough anymore:
To me you're just a big bully;
And, if you think I'm scared... not really:
You're just hot headed, and blowing off steam;
But, you need to come correct, and stop being mean:
Your own insecurities are driving you insane;
That's why you walking around calling
other people out of their name:
It seems to me that you are the one that's scared;
And, you're just a coward, that's what I heard:
You only pick on the ones that don't defend themselves;
And, you need an audience and you're never by yourself;
You're trying to prove a point, that you are big, and tough;

X-PRESSION

But, you're bothering innocent people, and enough's enough:
It's about time you're cut down to your rightful size;
And, you're very small this- I'm not surprised!
While, you were going around picking on others;
Now, it's your time to run for cover,
Be afraid of me, because I'm coming for you;
Then we'll see who's afraid of who.

Mother's Day...

For all the mothers in the house;
Who always shares and go without:
And is willing to give;
For your babies to live:
You didn't mind the sacrifice;
You never even thought twice:
Every day is Mother's Day;
As you sing to 'Our Father' with praise:
Thank you, Jesus, for blessing me;
With a gift of maternity:
You trusted me with this precious life;
Now I'm going to treat it right:
Please Lord let me be worthy of;
Teaching them about Jesus love:
A mother's willing to sacrifice;
For any, and all her children's life:
You're always there when they need you the most;
You never deny like other folks:
You go above and beyond to make them smile;
Even if it only lasts for a little while:
Your heart instantly breaks when your children are hurt;
You're always there and never dessert:
You will show your love if you're given a chance;
You work hard for your children with your bare hands:
You cook, clean, and sew;

X-PRESSION

And you better know, you do a whole lot more:
You read to them; you write with them;
And you always go out on a limb for them:
You make their beds and comb their heads;
And you always make sure that they're fed:
You wipe their nose, and clip their toes;
And you watch faithfully, to see where they go:
You teach them their first words when they begin to talk;
And you are a ball of nerves when they start to walk:
You take them to school on their first day;
And throughout the years you continue to pray:
You help them a lot in their time of need;
And sometimes they forget to say thank you, or please:
You don't mind your job, even though it's sometimes hard labor;
You know that you're truly blessed because
God showed you favor:
You watch them diligently as they grow up along the way;
You always remind them to worship and pray:
God has blessed you with the gift of life;
Sometimes they come without you being a wife:

If you have a mother, please cherish her dear;
And please remember to keep her near:
To all the mothers I say this with love;
You're truly blessed from our Father above!
And I'm truly grateful God had his way;
So, please enjoy your Mother's Day!

Wait Love...

A summer love that did not last;
It moved slowly and resolved fast:
Their hearts were one, for a little while;
They soon realized it cramped their style:
So, they both moved on to never return;
Willing to work hard for a love to earn:
They wanted a mate to call their own;
To love forever and make a home:
So, they decided to take a chance;
And, date around, before romance:
They wanted to wait until they were sure;
To, find a love that's true and pure:

There's plenty to choose from, state-to-state;
So try your best to avoid mistakes:
There's always someone willing to wait;
To give their love, at a later date:
So do your best, and take your time;
And, your true love, you'll eventually find.

Because...

They teased and mocked me;
Because they didn't know a thing about me:
They brought me pain;
Because of their insecurities and shame:
They didn't understand me;
Because they never stop to look and see:
I wasn't accepted;
Because of all the misconceptions:
I wasn't in the in-crowd;
Because I didn't yell, or speak out loud:
I never fit in;
Because they only pretended to be my friend;
I was never liked;
Because they always tried to start a fight:
I was falsely accused;
Because they refuse to follow the rules:
I was mistreated;
Because their lives weren't fulfilled,
I was ignored;
Because in life, they wanted more:
I was neglected;
Because in their days, they were rejected:
They never let up;
However, I didn't quit, or give up:
I was always denied;

Because of it, I was inspired:
I rose above, all their despair;
Because of it, I'm prosperous and secure:
Because of their very doubt;
God brought my talents out:
And because of my faith in Jesus;
I prayed and waited for my season.

The New Wave Boys...

Girls with the heart of a man;
I don't think the world quite understands:
All the rules have changed;
But, games remain:
Society forces their hands;
So, they stand together, and rise like a man:
I do believe that they're okay;
I just think they want their way:
Something's trapped inside of them;
That makes them need to be a him!
They're not the average girls, you see;
The "man" in them wants to go free!
They're more of a "man," then some men I know;
So, please don't call them a girl anymore,
They fight for dignity, and with pride;
Because of the "man" raging inside:
Just, watch carefully how they move;
The "swagger" they have is very smooth:
They'll snatch the girls and throw the guys off;
Cause of the words coming out their mouths:
So, be aware of "the new wave boys,"
They might just be a woman scorned!

Family Love...

A family is very precious to have;
They'll bring love and cheer, and lots of laughs:
If you're blessed to have one, cherish them please;
They're really here to help meet your needs:
It could be an aunt, sister, or a brother;
Maybe you have a cousin, uncle or your mother:
Whichever one works for you;
Get some advice on the things you do:
A father's love would be nice if he's there;
Give him the chance to show he cares:
A mother's love is sweet indeed;
She's always willing to house, and feed:
If you get a sister full of charm;
She'll never bring you any harm:
And a brother strength is like no other;
He's especially loyal; he's from your mother:
Now if you have a cousin or two;
They're always ready to groove with you:
Your aunts are especially really cool;
They'll help if you break the rules:
And if you have any uncles, they're alright;
They'll go the distance, and will help you fight:
Now when it comes to that grandmother;
Her bonds stronger than any lover:
You'll learn to hunt, and fish from your grandfather;
He stands strong, and proud, and is not a coward:

X-PRESSION

If you get a daughter or son;
The love continues, and so does the fun:
Families come in all types, and sizes;
Sometimes their unrelated, you'll be surprised:
You need to know about family love;
They're all a blessing from our Father above.

The Beautiful Black Woman...

The beautiful black woman has a lot to give;
Serving others is how she lives:
Her time is very precious indeed;
She gives it to others because of their needs:
Beautiful black women are caring and loyal to the very end;
When she's down for you, she's a special friend:
When you watch her, you'll see the beauty shine;
It's amazing how she's willing to swallow her pride:
Beautiful black woman, she'll give her all to the very last;
And she'll never judge you for your past:
She's the one that you need to keep by your side;
She's willing to be that "ride or die!"
Her beauty shines elegantly, among most;
Her charm separates her, from common folks:
Beautiful black woman, can't you tell;
Her skin is always glowing; it's never pail:
She nursed her babies from her breast;
Giving them nutrients and her best:
Beautiful black woman, feel her charm:
She'll wrap you in her loving arms:
Beautiful black woman, only a few remain;

X-PRESSION

The things she does, she'll bare no shame:
Beautiful black woman, her struggle is hard;
She's never willing to drop her guards;
Beautiful black woman, feel her pain;
She'll never let you forget her name.

Chapter 5

Entertsinmeny

1. 1. A Very Hot Day
2. Pretty, Petty, Penny-Pincher
3. Classy, County, Chick
4. I'm Sleepy
5. Bragging, Banging, Bingo, Buddies
6. Back in Time
7. From...The...To...The...
8. You Belong
9. Diddy...Wah...Diddy
10. Bunny Rabbit
11. Move the Waste
12. Can't Find Me
13. Talk to Myself
14. Ghetto Twisted

X-pression

A Very Hot Day…

I went with my family to the water park;
We stayed there, having fun until it got dark:
I was in the water relaxing or sitting in the sun;
Either way, I had lots of fun:
Some of us used squirters, and I played ball;
Then I sat back in a lounge chair, and watched the waterfall:
We were in the water slipping, and splashing;
My oldest son was even breakdancing;
My youngest son had a waterproof camera;
He swam around, taking pictures of the entire family:
Oh what laughs we got from that;
It was all fun and games, and that's a fact:
Then my granddaughter went down the water slide;
She asked me to go with her, but I was too big for the ride:
So I stood on the side and watched her play;
And we all had a wonderful day,
She cried "something terrible," when it was time to leave;
She screamed, "Daddy, can we stay a little longer, please"!
But, they were about to close, so we could no longer play;
Then I said, "Awe baby, we'll be back again on another hot day!"

Pretty, Petty, Penny-Pincher...

She's a pretty, petty, penny-pincher;
Now, why did you bring that cheapskate with you?
Everywhere we go she's counting change;
It is very annoying, and it's also strange:
She is always ordering, from the "dollar menu,"
And, she brings her soda with her:
She never stays for any dessert;
If she spends over budget, I think it hurts:
She has lots of money, and that's for sure;
Because she never spends it anywhere;
She can't take it with; doesn't she know;
She'll have to leave this earth, but it can't go:
Everyone calls her a stingy tightwad;
But, it doesn't matter to her, if they say it out loud:
She has very nice things in our home;
But she ordered them all, over the phone:
She can't stand the thought of spending cash;
It must be debited, or her life will crash:
It must be subtracted before she brings it home;
For if it's not, she won't spend it at all:
I think her money is plastered in her walls;

Because she's often scared to make a call:
Some friends stopped by to play cards for a while;
But, they couldn't read the numbers, because, it was the same deck she played with as a child:
So, they invited her to come out, and go to the show;
But, she said she could watch a movie on her phone, then she slammed the door!
She waits for the neighbor to throw out the paper;
And, she reads the news, a whole day later:
She keeps the lights off throughout her house;
And she sees by candles, as she moves about:
She doesn't have cable when she watches TV;
So, the only channel she gets is ABC:
She uses "Kool-Aid" to make makeup,
And, you can smell a fruity flavor, when you get near her:
She flushes her toilet once a day;
To make sure the water doesn't waste away:
She cares for her wounds at home, rather than going to a hospital;
Because, she refuses to pay a doctor to be in the middle:
She eats Ramen noodles from day to night;
And, she said the meat seasoning would be alright:
She rides her bike everywhere she goes;
She said "it will be too expensive, to buy a car, you know,"
She trades her clothing at the Goodwill;
Rather than buy new ones, and getting the bill:
I haven't met anyone else, who's that cheap yet;
She's a pretty petty penny-pincher, and one of a kind, I bet.

X-PRESSION

Classy, County, Chicks...

Two classy, county, chicks,
Took a ride in the city for a ghetto fix;
They had no idea the neighborhood they were in;
They were talking to different people, trying to make a friend:
A woman asked one of them if she could try on her shoes;
Then she cursed her out when she refused:
They went inside a building to use the restroom;
But they took a little too long to get through:
Because when they stepped outside;
Someone was stealing the tires right off their ride:
One man screamed at them, with the top of his voice;
And they took off running; they had no choice:
They both had a blank look on their face as if
they didn't know what to do;
Then they ran into a fugitive, they saw on the Channel 4 News:
They both took a deep breath and swallowed their pride;
And, said we need to call a cab and get us a ride:
One said to the other, "We need to go home";
At that very moment, someone snatched her phone:
Now they're scared-straight, walking down the road;
Huddling next to each other because they were getting cold;
The sun was going down; it was getting dark;
So, they decided to walk back to where the car was parked:

Jacqueline James

To, their surprise it was no longer there;
And, they look around to see if someone cared:
One of them sat on the curve and began to cry;
The other one said to her, "you better wipe your eyes
unless you want to die."
She said, "Girl, do you know where you're at? We're in the hood!
We ain't getting no sympathy; I thought you understood,"
So, they began to walk and talked among themselves;
Then they stole two kids bikes because it was the only thing left:
They pumped for hours until they finally made it home;
One looked at the other and said, "Girl the next time you want to
go to the city you're on your own!"
They will never again go where the people are slick;
Cause, they're not from the city, they're "Classy, County Chicks!"

X-PRESSION

I'm Sleepy...

I need to take some sleeping pills;
So, that I can lay down, rest, and chill:
My brain won't stop working;
And my mind just keeps lurking,
I'm tired as can be;
But sleep won't have me:
Now here's the deal;
I need some sleep for real:
I need to get some rest;
So, I can wake up and be my best:
My mind won't stop running;
And this here ain't funny:
My body's real tired;
And this feeling I can't hide;
My thoughts are going fast;
But my words are about to crash:
I'm starting to feel sick;
Cause I need to go to sleep quick:
I don't know what else to say;
Besides, I need to go to sleep today:
I need to hurry up and snore;
Because I can't take it no more:
I'm hurting in my head;
Cause I need to go to bed:

I got "the look,"
That I need a good night book,
Trust me; I won't peak,
I just need to get some sleep:
I'm very sad;
Because I need some sleep bad:
Sleep used to be my friend;
Now, 'you' don't comprehend:
Come on, and be kind;
And ease my mind:
Give me some peace;
So, I can get some wink:
I can sleep in a chair;
Or whatever's near:
I'll lay on the porch;
As long as sleep takes its course:
I don't need a bed;
I can sleep on my head:
I won't put up a fight;
Just let me sleep tonight:
I'm about to yell; "I'm sleepy, can't you tell?"

X-PRESSION

Bragging, Banging, Bingo, Buddies...

Bragging, banging, bingo, buddies,
They come out to play and get that money:
If the game of the day is Crazy Eight, to win;
It's better to play it with a friend:
They go to different places in the neighborhood;
They'll play every day if they could:
When they find a spot that they like;
They'll stay there and play from day to night:
It doesn't matter what the cost;
They've pouted over pennies when they've lost:
The two of them sit at the same table;
No one else sits there, because they're not able:
They cover the entire table; with all the boards, they play;
One play's 33, and the other plays 22,
and, they won't have it no other way:
They play 55 boards between the two;
And, they always know exactly what to do:
There are several different ways to play the game;
In order to win the rules may change:
It's 4 Corners or Crazy 8;

JACQUELINE JAMES

Or just plain old Bingo played straight:
Sometimes they win and sometimes they don't;
Nevertheless, they love the thought:
The bets start from pennies and go up;
And on certain days, they play for big bucks:
Win or not, they simply love the game;
Without it, their days won't be the same:
And when they win, they brag a lot;
Which makes you wish that you came out:
Every time you see them, they're together;
Going to different Bingo games in all types of weather:
They take a chance to win that money;
Cause they're bragging, banging, bingo, buddies.

X-PRESSION

Back in Time...

My mother reminisced, thinking back in time;
When to get in the theaters only cost a dime;
She could sit in the show, and watch movies all day long;
As long as she was willing to bring her kid sister along:
And, it was free to get in the neighborhood pools;
They will go swimming in the morning
and leave late in the afternoon:
All the payphones on the street corners were five cents to use;
You can talk for an hour about any type of news:
Public transportation cost you $0.15 to ride;
You could use it from day to night;
rather it was hot or cold outside:
And if you own a car, and needed to pay for gas;
You can spend a couple of bucks and ride all week; it'll last:
The cars ran good, and didn't break down a lot;
The worst that happened, they overheated if they got too hot:
You can pay $3 and feed a family of four;
They'll be full for the day and won't need to eat anymore:
People were honest, and you can leave your front door open;
There wasn't anyone stealing, and doing all that "doping,"
The children were obedient and filled with Christian values;
They knew if they acted out, their parents weren't having it:
They could be disciplined by any adult around;
And, that made them think twice before they decided to clown:
You could always find a job; the whole city stayed busy;

People work day and night until their heads became dizzy:
Everything was closed on Sundays; they all went to church to pray;
And it made their lives a lot richer throughout the weekdays:
You can smell some good cooking;
From every kitchen if you were looking:
You'll always get fed if you went to anybody's house;
You can get mashed potatoes,
cornbread, or spaghetti with meat sauce:
Their hospitality was remarkable and filled with "southern charm;"
Everybody was willing to lend a hand and never did any harm:
Children could stay out late, without the fear of being attacked;
The only fights that were seen, was
when the parents were talking smack:
The police were all friendly,
and always gave the children baseball cards;
And they got the children out the street, to play in their yards:
And all the school teachers work hard, and were very dedicated;
They went that extra mile, to make
sure the children were well-educated:
A $100 was good for any family to have;
That meant good living, health insurance,
and a well covered dental plan:
No one even counted to a million because
you couldn't spend it in a lifetime;
And the rich who had that much made sure their children, grand-children, and great-grandchildren were fine:
And the air was so clean and pure; you could live outdoors;
It wasn't filled with gas and pollutants and a whole lot more:
I thanked her for this history lesson,
to know what would have been;
If we weren't filled with lust and greed, and making enemies in-stead of friends:
She said that she doesn't know where these changes stemmed
from, but it's messing up our days;
And her best advice for this generation, we must continue to pray!

X-PRESSION

From-The...To...The...

From the bottom to the top;
The crap doesn't stop:
The front to the back;
It's all full of smack:
From the beginning to the end;
They just must win:
From the open to the close;
It's whatever goes:
From the up to the down;
They'll soon come around:
From the in to the out;
They'll all move about:
From the rich to the poor;
They'll need a little more
From around and around;
They won't make a sound:
From the trust to the doubt;
That's what it's all about;
From the glad to the sad:
They're all getting mad:
From fast to slow;
They're all on the go:
From sick to healed;

They all knew the deal:
From quick to fast;
It's all going to last:
From the enemies to the friends;
We'll all do it again.

You Belong…

Come on baby wash my dishes, and scrub my floors,
you know you belong:
Wash my clothes, and cook my food, make yourself at home:
Make my bed now, wash my walls and don't you take too long;
Brush my hair, and rub my back, and get off the dog-on-phone!
Shine my shoes and dust my room;
And make sure you take care of it soon:
I'm going to work and, I won't be gone long;
And make sure you clean the place good while I'm gone:
I want you to wash my car when I return;
And if you don't know how to shine the tires, you will learn:
Now, go fill my tank up, so I can take it for a spin;
It needs to be ready when it's time for me to go again:
You better not pout or give me no lip;
You know what time it is, so don't even trip:
I'm coming in the house so fix my plate;
Or it's going to be a problem if my dinner is late;
I'm done, now clean this kitchen;
And, make sure you sweep and mop; Are you listening?
I'm tired now, so run my bath;
Come here and wash my back, and my upper half;
Dry me off good and get my feet;

I'm about to lay down and get me some sleep:
Don't lay here and get comfortable with me;
you ain't done nothing all day;
The little stuff you did was "child's play!"
Get your butt up and clean this room;
Don't you know it's about to be morning soon:
For dinner tonight, I want you to cook me a pot roast;
But right now, you need to start on my breakfast,
and don't you burn my toast!
While I'm gone, clean out the garage and vacuum the rug;
Get off of me; you don't need a hug!
No, you're not going anywhere to have fun;
And you bet not get on the phone, to call no one:
You don't get a life outside of me;
Taking care of me is where you're meant to be!
Now, don't be singing that same old song;
Get it together; you know you belong.

Diddy...Wah...Diddy...

We went shopping way out in "Diddy-Wah-Diddy,"
Where things are nice, clean,
and pretty:
The air was crisp, and the sun was shining;
The babies were laughing, and the children were mining:
The people were friendly and all full of life;
And the men were walking along the side of their wives:
Items in this thrift store were all clean and nice;
They were hung up neatly with a reasonable price:
I decided to stay and shop for a while;
Because all the people greeted me with a smile:
I bought lots of things that I thought I might need;
I would've bought them all, but I couldn't show my greed:
So, I shopped around and bought the most useful items;
And the bargains I got, made my day a lot brighter:
My mother and my Godmother also came along;
They were both satisfied singing a happy song:
And on the way home we all agreed;
The shopping was a lot better way out in "Diddy-Wah-Diddy!"

Bunny Rabbit…

Bunny rabbit, bunny rabbit, hop, hop, hop;
When I see you coming the fun don't stop:
Eating in my garden to feed your babies;
Eating up all my cabbage and driving me crazy:
Come on now and work with me little bunny;
I need to feed my family too and this isn't funny:
I don't want to ruin it, by putting poison down;
I like to see your family playing and hopping all around:
You breed a lot and have plenty of babies, fast as can be;
I can't possibly count you all; you're too many for my eyes to see:
I watch you hop in and out of my bushes and play all day long;
It's probably 50 or more of you, or my numbers could be wrong:
Nevertheless, you eat my vegetables and never say a word;
And when I scream "get out of there,"
you act as if you hadn't heard:
You look so cute at Easter time dressed up in "chocolate wraps,"
The kids eat all the eggs and candy from their
baskets and have a bunny left:
We all know you never laid an egg and aren't even capable of that;
However, it's still a fun tradition, and I'm just stating a fact,
Little bunny you're so cute, and darling as can be;
But I need you to stay out of my garden
and save some vegetables for me.

Move the Waste...

You know when you got to go;
When you can't hold it no more:
Please don't hold that dookie in;
Cause your bowels are your best friend:
Now, don't seat up and pout;
If you can't get that crap out:
Go lay down on your side, not your stomach or your back;
Lay there for awhile until your food digest:
If you can't get out, what you put inside;
Then you need to change your diet:
If it doesn't help at all;
Then take a laxative, or make a call:
If your bowels, suddenly stop;
Then, you know they're about to lock:
You need to get it out of you;
Whatever's trapped inside of you:
If you don't you'll be wearing a bag;
And, it'll be horrible, and awfully sad:
When you go the doctor for your check-up;
But he really can't tell you what's up:
If the doctors can't give you a straight answer;
Then that means you probably got that cancer!
Now, you're praying real hard, but there's nothing they could do,
Besides give you medication and make it comfortable for you:

So, your family must be aware;
If you can't move the waste from out of there!
We all must move our waste to survive;
In order to stay alive.

Can't Find Me...

You can't find me; I wear many disguises;
My hair is green, and I wear big lashes,
I wear false nails as long as can be;
I have a tat, didn't you see:
I wear my pants off my waste;
And lots of makeup on my face:
My hair is long full of weave;
It's green and gold I do believe:
I wear high heels, and I walk real fast;
They're tall as stilts, but I don't crash:
I wear skinny jeans, and they're very tight;
I don't wear them during the day, but I'll wear them at night:
My shirt is loose, to show my breast;
It's tight at the bottom, and covers the rest:
I wear a big hat on my head;
But, I prefer to wear a hoodie instead:
I have a dress that I wear outside;
But, it doesn't go down pass by thighs:
I have a suit and a jacket too
I like to wear them cause they're new:
I have a long puffy wig;
That I only wear to a gig,
I have some braids in my hair;

Jacqueline James

If you don't like them, I don't care
I wear tennis shoes, and a sports jacket;
Sometimes I make noise and put up a racket:
I wear silk shirts with short skirts;
I like to hang out late and flirt:
Sometimes I'm quiet and calm as can be;
I'm incognito if you are looking for me,
I told you I have many disguises;
And that's the reason you can't find me.

X-PRESSION

Talk to Myself...

I'll tell you what, if I get writer's block;
I'll just talk to myself until it stops:
I know between me and myself;
We can find something interesting left,
We can talk to each other all day long;
And I'll let me know if I'm right or wrong:
Between the two of us we'll have a lot to say;
It'll help me write and brighten our day:
She lets me know what's on her mind;
And I'll tell her when I'm doing fine:
She cheers me up when I'm feeling low;
And I let her know when I don't need it anymore:
She's my best friend you must believe;
And she's the only friend I'll ever need,
I make her better, and she makes me great;
And sometimes we stay up talking late:
I look in the mirror to see her face;
And she quickly puts me in my place:
I sometimes think if she's alright;
And she keeps me up wondering throughout the night:
She really is a sight to see;
And I'm feeling good because she's admiring me:

Jacqueline James

So, I let her know that I'm doing fine;
I'm in her head, and she's in mine:
We talk to each other just for fun;
And we laugh out loud when we're done:
I talk to myself everywhere I go;
And answer me so I'll know:
When people ask, "who are you talking to?"
I respond, "I'm talking to me; I'm not talking to you!"

Ghetto Twisted...

Check yourself, before you wreck yourself;
Making something good, from the hood;
I thought you understood:
While you watering for this money;
Don't try to count my pockets, honey:
I'm an honest person, so don't lie to me;
I'll kill you; you can get it, you'll get it free:
In my pocket is my gun;
Pow, pow, pow,
Don't try to run; your butt is done:
I'll make you drip, drip, drip;
Don't you trip!
I look good, I talk good, but don't get it twisted,
I'm still from the hood:
Rapping, dancing, getting it in;
Man, keep it moving, we ain't friends:
What you on man?
You ain't bout that life;
Last I checked, you were on strike:
I'm laid back, and I'm cool;
Cause I'm that real dude:
While we in these streets;

Don't try to one-up me:
Man, it's all on you;
Make it do-what-it-do!
Don't get it twisted, make it happen, captain!

X-pression

Chapter 6

Special Dedication
1. My Friend
2. Baby 'Angel'
3. Message from Heaven
4. Happy Anniversary
5. My Heart
6. New Friend

My Friend...

All of the qualities of a true friend, you possess;
As a friend of mine, you're one of the best,
Under any circumstances we could've met;
And we still would've been friends, I bet:
Your spirit radiates a pleasant glow;
And it's sure to bring about smiles, wherever you go:
I don't know much about you; you know;
However, I'm pleased with the things you show:
You don't have to be with someone every day to be their friend;
You just need to appreciate the kindness
that they're willing to lend:
I'm glad to have met your acquaintance;
When I see you, your presence makes my day a little brighter:
Thank you for all the kindness you've shown;
And as a friend, I'm happy to say, you're my own:
I hope that I made you blush with this simple poem;
Because I intended to turn on my charm.
Dedicated to: Harry

JACQUELINE JAMES

Baby Angel sread your wings;
You've gone home to sing for the King:
You will be missed, but you're not needed here;
You're with the Master, have no fear:
Your job has been assigned to watch over us;
From up in the heavens with God we trust:
You'll sing his praise to start our day;
And, watch us faithfully along the way;
We'll worship gracefully until the moon gives her light;
And you'll keep us peacefully throughout our night;
Now, baby angel spread your wings;
We'll start our day, as you begin to sing;
You'll sing with the love our Savior brings:
You give us joy throughout our day;
And, we'll remember your smile along the way:
Our nights are kept safely as you stay;
And God's promise is fulfilled as we pray;
Baby angel spread your wings out wide;
So that we may feel your love from inside:
You bring us hope in our day;
And, from God's word, we will not stray:
Help us to see the mercy God gives;
So our souls may be free in order to live:
Baby angel spread your wings;
Now we'll watch you fly;
Watching over us from the sky!

X-PRESSION

Message from Heaven...

Grandma, grandma, remember me,
I'm the little angel, in your heart!
And because of it, we'll never be apart:
I'm not gone, I'm waiting on you;
We'll be together again, real soon:
Grandma, I'm up in heaven hanging out;
I'm not sad, and there's no need to doubt:

Now, stop that crying, I'm okay!
I'm up in heaven, where I'm going to stay:
God has me in the comfort of his arms;
I'm safe, I'm happy, and I'm very warm:
It's so peaceful Grandma; I'm doing fine;
I'm just hanging out with our Father, cause he's mine:

I love you Grandma, and I know you love me;
But right now, I'm in the place; I need to be:
I know you miss me, I miss you too;
But, you must stay there for a while, there's too much to do;
You must make sure all the family has Christian values;
So, when their time comes, Jesus will have them!
And, we'll all be reunited in this Holy Place;
And we'll be blessed forever, to see our Father's face!

Message from Heaven: Keshawn

P.S. Give hugs and kisses to all our family and friends; may they stay in perfect peace, until we meet again!
Love,
Keshawn

My Heart...

When the rain falls, I think of you;
When it's sunny outside, you're there too:
When the snow is there as pure as can be;
The love is true for you and me:
When the leaves are golden from the autumn air;
I'll still be there to show I care:
When the sea rises greatly and heavily the wind blows;
Where are you? But with me, for together we'll grow:
When the night comes, and the stars shine bright;
Remembering my love for you takes me through the night;

Dedicated to: Sherece Whitehorn

1

Happy Anniversary...

Today Bishop Melvin James Smith and first Lady Jacqueline Smith
are celebrating their 12 years in ministry.

Our congregation are truly blessed,
to worship up under such holiness,
We thank you, Jesus, for all you've done;
Because of their faithfulness, some souls were won:
They're very much appreciated throughout our congregation;
They're always ready to serve, in any situation:
Their hard work and dedication is what keeps them going;
And true humility is what they're always showing:
It's an honor to worship under their leadership;
We're very inspired as our spirits are lifted,
I speak for us all when I say they're loved;
And, they're a blessing to many, from our Father above:

So, congratulations on your anniversary;
God has blessed you and shown you mercy.

X-PRESSION

New Friend...

I met a new friend, who's a poet like myself;
She sings from her soul until there's nothing left:
The night our paths crossed, it was truly meant;
She's a remarkable person, who's heavenly sent:
As a friend, I'm blessed to have her;
She's filled with love and Christian values:
We went to brunch to share our poems;
It was a pleasure just to see her charm:
Her words were filled with hope and joy;
She remains inspired when times are hard:
We came out to mingle despite the weather;
God had His reasons for bringing us together:
We talked, laughed, and shared our stories;
We sat through a storm, but had no worries:
God placed an anointing on her life;
She's a special woman, mother, and wife:
It's very important to me to have her as a friend;
From all her talent, that she's willing to lend:
To get better acquainted was our main objective;
We talked for hours, without any distractions:
We both discovered that we have kindred spirits;
God has blessed us through grace, for the world to hear us:
Our friendship is filled with promise because it's new;
And I'm praying she feels the same way too.
Dedicated to: Tianna Smith

JACQUELINE JAMES

X-PRESSION

www.ingramcontent.com/pod-product-compliance
Lightning Source LLC
Chambersburg PA
CBHW052159110526
44591CB00012B/2006